Ian & Fred's

BIG GREEN BOOK

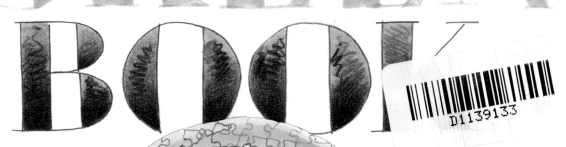

Written by
Fred Pearce

Illustrated by
Ian Winton

Foreword by
James Lovelock

Kingfisher Books

Ian and Fred's Big Green Book was inspired by the Gaia hypothesis. This is a theory put forward by James Lovelock, a British scientist. He suggests that all living things (known as the biosphere) are linked, and have created and maintained the right atmosphere and other conditions they need for their survival.

We humans, however, are altering the atmosphere, the soil and the oceans with our pollution, and destroying plants and animals. The Gaia theory helps you understand why it is important for us to live in harmony with our planet in order to survive, as Dr Lovelock explains in his foreword.

FOREWORD

In many ways Earth is like a living thing, but not quite alive like you or me. Like our breath and blood, the air and water are kept wonderfully constant so that all the parts of Earth are nourished.

Have you ever looked at a tree stump and seen the rings marking a year of the tree's life? The outer ring is the bark that surrounded and protected the soft ring of living tissue immediately beneath it. Inside are lots of rings of wood. The bark and wood of the tree are both dead, but they were once living cells.

Earth is like a tree. On the outside is the atmosphere, the layer that protects us from the cold and alien perils of space. Beneath the air is the biosphere - the zone of living things - trees, plants, animals, fish, most importantly the microscopic creatures of the soil and ocean, and of course, people. Under the soil and seas are hard rocks. The whole ensemble of air, ocean, biosphere and rocks go to make the living Earth.

What would the Earth be like if it were dead? It would be like Mars or Venus or the Moon, with a bone-dry, bare rock surface, because oceans don't last on a dead planet. There would be no life-giving oxygen in the air and nowhere could you light a fire.

Live Earth is a warm and comfortable home that has stayed that way for more than three and a half billion years. The author, William Golding, suggested that I call it Gaia after the old Greek goddess of Earth. The name Gaia is also now the name of the theory I invented to explain why the Earth is nearly always comfortable for its inhabitants, whatever they may be. I hope that you will enjoy this book as much as I did. I hope too that you will find the Gaia theory helps to understand our amazing and wonderful planet.

James E Lovelock.

CONTENTS

THE GOLDILOCKS PLANET

Earth is one of nine planets that circle the Sun. So far as we know, Earth is the only planet that is home to living things. Earth and its nearest neighbours, Mars and Venus, were formed at about the same time, in the same way, and from the same sorts of rocks. So why is there life on Earth but nowhere else?

One reason is the heat from the Sun - what we call sunlight. Without it, neither plants nor animals could live. Venus is much closer to the Sun than Earth, and it receives much more heat. The temperature on the surface of Venus is over 450° C, hotter than a kitchen oven at its hottest. Mars and the other planets further away from the Sun receive much less heat than Earth. Living on Mars would be like living inside a freezer - very, very cold.

Like the bowl of porridge that Goldilocks ate in the story of the Three Bears, the temperature on Earth is not too hot, not too cold, but just right for life.

Neptune

Jupiter

Saturn

Mars

Mercury

Venus

Sun

Earth

Moon

Venus is too hot...

Mars is too cold...

but Earth is just right for life to flourish.

Pluto

Uranus

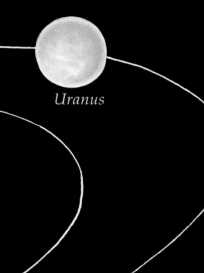

Carbon dioxide acts like an invisible blanket, holding in some of the heat from the Sun.

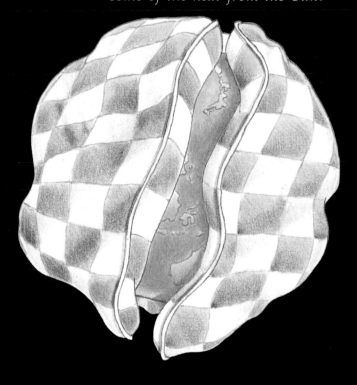

The atmosphere, the thick layer of gases that surrounds our planet, is another reason for life on Earth. It is made up mostly of nitrogen, some oxygen and a little carbon dioxide and water vapour. We use oxygen to breathe, but carbon dioxide is also essential for life on Earth. It acts like a blanket wrapped around the planet, absorbing some of the heat from the Sun. Venus has a very thick blanket of carbon dioxide that keeps it very hot. Mars has very little carbon dioxide to keep the heat in. If Earth had no atmosphere, it would be like Mars - freezing cold, with a temperature of around -20° C.

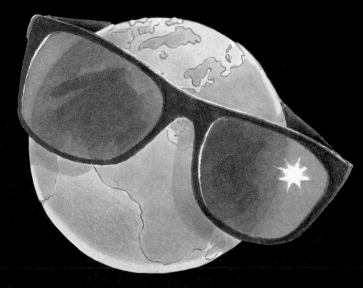

Although we need the Sun to live, some of its rays are harmful to us. Strong, invisible rays, called ultraviolet radiation, cause sunburn and can increase our chances of getting skin cancer and other diseases. But part of our atmosphere, high above Earth, protects us by blocking out most of the harmful ultraviolet radiation. We call this part of the atmosphere the ozone layer. No living thing on the surface of our planet could survive without its protection.

The ozone layer acts like a pair of sunglasses, blocking out harmful ultraviolet radiation.

A BUMPY RIDE

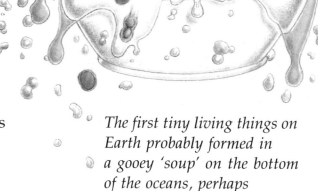

Earth was formed about 5 thousand million years ago. The first living things on it were tiny organisms on the bottom of the oceans. They appeared about 4 thousand million years ago. Living things have not always found it easy to survive on Earth. But, like a spinning top, our living planet has recovered every time it has been knocked off balance.

The first tiny living things on Earth probably formed in a gooey 'soup' on the bottom of the oceans, perhaps 4 thousand million years ago.

About 2 thousand million years ago, some tiny floating plants called algae began to make oxygen. First, oxygen collected in the oceans. Then it started to bubble up out of the water and, for the first time, there was oxygen in the atmosphere. The algae changed the atmosphere of Earth.

About one thousand million years ago, living things moved from water onto land.

Many of the tiny organisms in the oceans were killed by oxygen. It was poisonous to them. But the oxygen allowed others, including those that produced the oxygen, to evolve and grow. Sunlight turned some of the oxygen in the air into ozone, which is a special form of oxygen. With oxygen to breathe and an ozone layer to protect them from harmful radiation from the sun, the first plants and animals moved ashore less than a thousand million years ago.

Several times in Earth's history, catastrophes have come from outer space. Every few million years, comets - some the size of a large town - hurtle towards our planet from the far side of our galaxy. Occasionally, they crash into Earth.

The biggest comet may have crashed into our planet 250 million years ago. The crash seems to have made the oceans boil and huge fires rage. Most types of living things died out. But within a few million years, the atmosphere and the oceans recovered and entirely new types of animals, including the predecessors of dinosaurs, evolved.

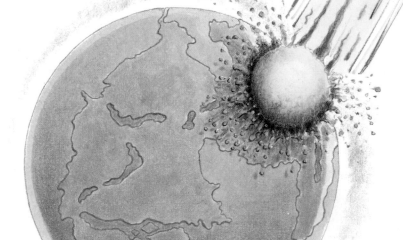

Comets, the size of entire cities, have crashed into Earth several times.

Another comet may have hit Earth 65 million years ago. Many scientists think that it set the planet on fire and killed off half of all living things, including dinosaurs. Many small animals survived, however. They evolved over millions of years into the animals - human beings included - that we know today.

Human-like creatures first walked on Earth about 2 million years ago. It was about then that a slight wobble in the planet's orbit around the Sun started the first Ice Age. Sheets of ice spread out from the North Pole until they covered large parts of the planet, including land where cities such as London, New York and Berlin now stand. Eventually, the ice retreated. But the wobble has caused several more Ice Ages since then and, each time, the ice has killed off many types of plants and animals. In a few thousand years' time, your home might be buried beneath a layer of ice several kilometres thick.

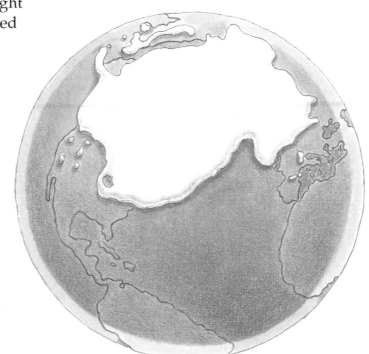

About 2 million years ago, a slight wobble in the orbit of Earth around the Sun caused ice sheets to spread across the planet.

Despite Earth's bumpy ride through time, our planet has always remained a place where life can survive. But today, life on Earth may be facing its greatest threat - from one of its newest creatures - human beings.

Modern man casts a long shadow across the future of living things on Earth.

THE GREAT BALANCING ACT

When Earth formed it was extremely hot. As the molten rocks on the surface of the planet cooled, they created a thin crust on the surface. Gradually, over millions of years, an atmosphere formed. It was composed of gases pumped out from the molten interior of the planet through volcanoes. That atmosphere was very unlike our modern atmosphere. It had no oxygen and was composed almost entirely of carbon dioxide. The carbon dioxide and other gases trapped enough of the Sun's heat to keep Earth warm. These gases are known as the greenhouse gases because they hold in heat from the Sun, rather like the panes of glass in a greenhouse.

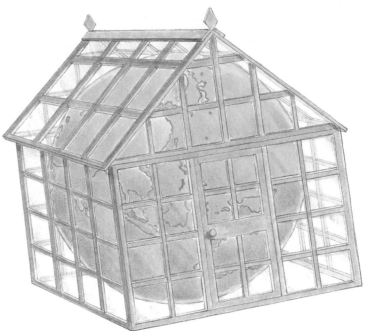

Like the glass windows in a greenhouse, gases, such as carbon dioxide, trap the Sun's heat and keep us warm.

When the atmosphere first formed, the Sun was not nearly as hot as today. So you might expect that the temperature on Earth would have been freezing cold. In fact, scientists have found evidence from fossils of living things from three thousand million years ago, which shows that the climate was more or less the same as now. Despite ups and downs in temperature, such as the Ice Ages, Earth has never become too hot or too cold for life to carry on.

When it first formed, our atmosphere was 98 per cent carbon dioxide.

How has the climate stayed so stable? The secret may lie with the greenhouse gases. When the Sun was cooler, the atmosphere was 98 per cent carbon dioxide. But as the Sun has become gradually hotter, the amount of carbon dioxide in the air has decreased dramatically to less than 1 per cent today. It's as if Earth has been able to shed several layers of thick blankets to keep its temperature constant. But where has all the carbon gone?

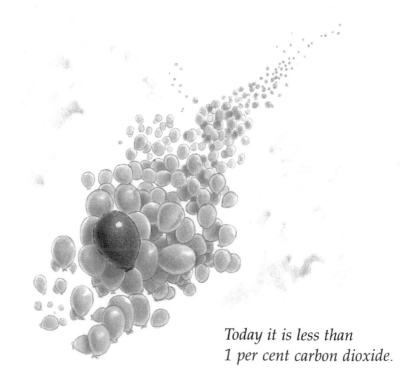

Today it is less than 1 per cent carbon dioxide.

Over hundreds of millions of years the carbon dioxide in the planet's early atmosphere has been absorbed by most living things, especially those in the oceans. They use the carbon to grow and make tissue and skeletons. When they die, their remains fall to the ocean floor where, eventually, they form new rock. Living things have played an important role in controlling the planet's temperature. Without them, there would be much more carbon dioxide in the air - and our planet would be much hotter.

Living things keep our environment fit for life, by controlling the amount of chemicals in air and water. They keep the amount of salt in the oceans from rising too high, for instance. They also keep a constant control on oxygen in the air. For hundreds of millions of years, roughly a quarter of our atmosphere has been made up of oxygen. If the amount rose, fires would quickly spread across the planet. This is because fires burn much faster where there is more oxygen. But if there were much less oxygen, most living things, including humans, would suffocate.

Oxygen is constantly being destroyed in the air by sunlight. But it is replaced by plants, which manufacture oxygen. Without plants, the atmosphere would soon run out of oxygen.

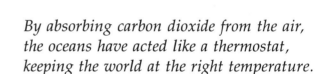

By absorbing carbon dioxide from the air, the oceans have acted like a thermostat, keeping the world at the right temperature.

Our atmosphere performs a constant balancing act. Too much oxygen and we would all burn up ... too little and we would suffocate.

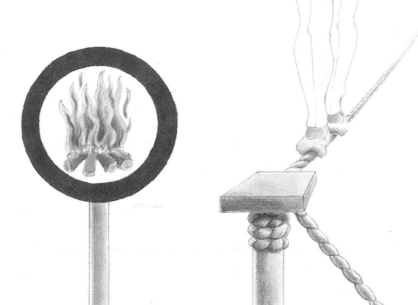

THE HUMAN FOOTPRINT

Modern man, known as Homo sapiens, evolved about 40,000 years ago, during the last Ice Age. But it is only within the last 10,000 years that man has tamed and altered the environment by planting crops, keeping animals and building towns and cities. 10,000 years ago the world population was about 10 million. Since then, it has increased fairly steadily, but it surges occasionally when humans find new ways to feed more people. Over the past 250 years, the population has grown from 5 hundred million to around 5 thousand million people.

Imagine humans as a load pulled by an engine, called Earth. When there were only a few million humans, the engine had no problem. But now it has 5 thousand million people to pull and its fuel - the natural resources we all need - may be running low.

ACQUIRED BY MANKIND Inc.

Even though the current population increase is beginning to slow down, scientists estimate that there will be 10 thousand million people on the planet by the year 2100. Each year there are another 80 million people on Earth, all needing food and shelter. When fewer people were using trees for fuel, diverting rivers to water fields, and mining the land, there was little damage to the environment. Now that humans have taken over most of the available land, the damage is worldwide. There are human footprints wherever we look - roads through rainforests, oil rigs in the Arctic, and cattle ranchers' fences where animals were once free to roam. As people take over land for farms and cities, they destroy plants and animals - who knows how many of these we might need in the future?

Homo sapiens is taking over the planet. There are very few untouched places left, such as the middle of rainforests, deserts and Antarctica.

More and more roads are built to link towns, ports and countries. They often criss-cross untouched land.

Farmers need to grow more and more food to feed all the thousands of millions of people. Recently, scientists have developed new types of cereals which ripen more quickly and produce more grain. But these crops need fertilizers to grow well, and pesticides to kill pests and prevent disease. These chemicals, in turn, upset the natural balance of insects and animals which live on and around the crops.

Farmers now grow twice as much food as they did thirty years ago, on the same amount of land.

In many places, soils have lost their natural goodness, because farmers can plough their land year after year in order to increase the amount that they grow. Eventually the soil becomes like dust and is blown away by the wind or washed away by rain. In the highlands of Ethiopia, farmers lose an estimated 3 thousand million tonnes of soil each year. They can no longer feed their families. In this way, many African farms are turning into desert.

When farmers overuse their land, the top layer of fertile soil starts to peel away.

The pesticides and fertilizers that farmers use interfere with the chemistry of soils. The farmers may get a bumper crop for a few years, but in time even the best fields may turn into deserts.

13

Most of Earth's resources are used by enormous cities. Their populations are growing all the time, creating huge megacities. Each has over 10 million inhabitants - more than the entire population of the whole world just 10,000 years ago. By the year 2000, there will be more than 25 megacities and almost half of the world population will be city dwellers. Particularly in poor countries, thousands of people move into cities each year, hoping to find work. Most fail, and live in shanty towns on the edge of the cities, often without proper housing, water supplies or sewage systems.

The rest of the world is being ruined in order to feed, clothe and house the people in these giant megacities. Mexico City, the world's largest city, may look like a tiny spot on a map of Mexico, but its 19 million inhabitants eat more than half the food produced in Mexico, use more than half its oil, and drive more than half its cars. Three-quarters of the people in China live in the country, but big cities like Beijing use three-quarters of all the country's electricity.

Megacities are growing all over the world.

Megacities dig and drill into the land for metals, fuel, and building materials.

Megacities have nowhere to put their waste except into the surrounding sea and countryside.

As megacities advance, wild animals flee and countryside is destroyed.

WATER - THE SPRING OF LIFE

It is curious that we called our planet 'Earth' when, in fact, over 70 per cent of it is covered with water. Water is essential to life. Without it neither plants nor animals could survive. But almost all the world's water is in the oceans, where it is salty and of little use to humans. Less than 3 per cent is fresh water and most of that is frozen in the polar icecaps or glaciers. Amazingly, less than 1 per cent of the world's water is found in rivers, lakes, or underground, where we can make use of it.

There will never be any more fresh water than there is now. No new water is made and water cannot escape from Earth. The water we use is recycled over and over again. As the Sun heats the seas and lakes, millions of litres of water rise into the air as invisible water vapour. This is known as evaporation. As the vapour rises, it cools and turns back into tiny water droplets, forming clouds, some of which are blown inland. The droplets join together - this is called condensation. Eventually, they fall as rain. The rain runs off the land into rivers, which eventually flow back into the sea, and the cycle is repeated.

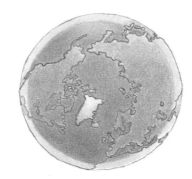

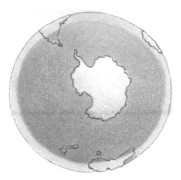

Most of the world is covered by water.

The natural water cycle

clouds form

rain falls

water flows back to the sea

water evaporates

This natural plumbing system is absolutely vital for life on Earth, yet we are poisoning more and more of this precious fresh water by pouring dangerous pollutants into rivers. When the water evaporates into the air, the pollution is left behind. Human sewage is a major pollutant, particularly in many parts of Africa, Asia and South America, where people do not have enough clean water for all their needs. They use the same pond, lake or river for washing, drinking, and as a toilet. Human sewage contains bacteria and viruses that cause deadly diseases. Although many countries treat sewage to make it less dangerous, in other places, untreated sewage is poured directly into rivers or the sea.

Our precious freshwater supply is being increasingly polluted.

Water is polluted in many other ways. Industrial waste is often poured deliberately into rivers. It may also leak accidentally from waste tips or underground storage tanks. Rain often washes pesticides into rivers. These chemicals seep through the soil to natural underground reservoirs of pure drinking water, which people reach by digging wells or drilling boreholes. If this water is polluted, the poisons stay there forever. Some cities are now spending thousands of millions of pounds to clean up water made unsafe by such pollution.

Dangerous metals, such as mercury and lead have been buried underground. These waste dumps are like toxic time bombs, because no-one knows when their poison might seep into the underground reservoirs from which millions of people take their drinking water.

Dams allow the flow of water to be controlled. They provide a store of water, and can help prevent flooding.

Over the last fifty years, people have built dams across some of the world's largest rivers. The water behind a dam forms a lake. Although dams have been useful for generating electricity and watering the land to grow crops, they have also caused problems. Before they were dammed, the rivers brought fine soil, called silt, downstream from the mountains. The silt naturally fertilized the land each year when the rivers flooded. Dams prevent the silt from flowing downstream, so that the farmers there have to buy artificial fertilizer. The silt settles at the bottom of the lake behind the dam, making the dam less efficient.

Rivers also carry salt from mountain rocks. Normally they carry the salt straight into the sea. When a dam diverts the water on to fields, the crops absorb the water, leaving the salt in the soil. Crops cannot grow in salty soil, so scientists are now looking at ways to wash the soil clean, and to develop plants that can tolerate salt.

In parts of India, Pakistan, Mexico and the United States, fields are now covered with a white crust of salt and are useless for growing crops.

For a long time, people thought it didn't matter how much waste was dumped in the oceans. They believed the oceans were so big that the waste would disperse harmlessly. Now they know better. Many coastal waters, where the water is shallow and rich in marine life, are becoming contaminated with sewage, chemicals and rubbish. Leaks from oil tankers can leave a thin slick of oil, many kilometres across, on the surface of an ocean.

Poisoning the water cycle

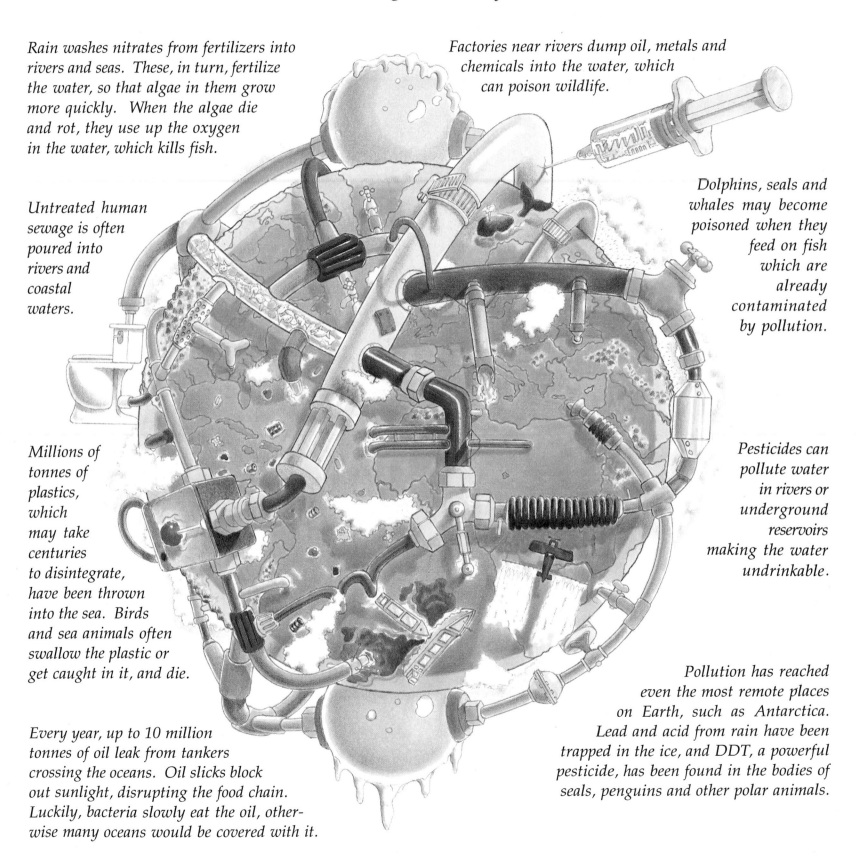

Rain washes nitrates from fertilizers into rivers and seas. These, in turn, fertilize the water, so that algae in them grow more quickly. When the algae die and rot, they use up the oxygen in the water, which kills fish.

Factories near rivers dump oil, metals and chemicals into the water, which can poison wildlife.

Untreated human sewage is often poured into rivers and coastal waters.

Dolphins, seals and whales may become poisoned when they feed on fish which are already contaminated by pollution.

Millions of tonnes of plastics, which may take centuries to disintegrate, have been thrown into the sea. Birds and sea animals often swallow the plastic or get caught in it, and die.

Pesticides can pollute water in rivers or underground reservoirs making the water undrinkable.

Every year, up to 10 million tonnes of oil leak from tankers crossing the oceans. Oil slicks block out sunlight, disrupting the food chain. Luckily, bacteria slowly eat the oil, otherwise many oceans would be covered with it.

Pollution has reached even the most remote places on Earth, such as Antarctica. Lead and acid from rain have been trapped in the ice, and DDT, a powerful pesticide, has been found in the bodies of seals, penguins and other polar animals.

THE WORLD IN A DUSTBIN

Every human contributes to the state of our planet. Some people, however, do far more damage than others. People who live in rich, industrialised countries consume most of the world's limited resources. They mine more metals to make everything from cars to drinks cans. They burn more oil to run their cars. They use more gas and electricity to light and heat their homes. They eat more food and chop down more forests for wood and paper. A quarter of the world's people consume three-quarters of the world's resources. The United States alone burns a quarter of the world's coal and oil each year, and uses more than a quarter of the world's dwindling stocks of aluminium and copper.

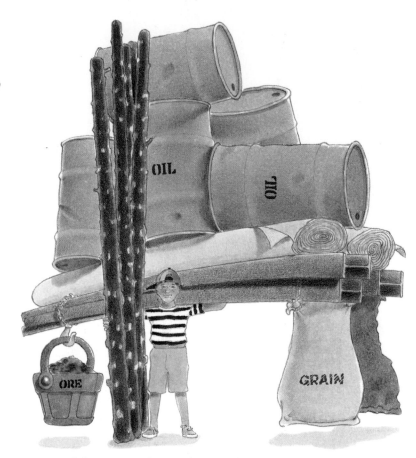

Many people worry about the extra numbers of children being born in poorer countries, but one child in an industrialised country consumes as much as 10 children in a poorer country.

A typical family may produce 50 kilograms of rubbish every week. That's more than 2 tonnes a year.

In the 'throw-away societies' of Europe and North America, most waste is poured down the drain, thrown on to the street, or left out for the refuse truck. More than a third of what we throw away is paper or cardboard. In our lifetime, each of us may throw away 50 tonnes of rubbish, including paper made from more than 200 trees.

People who live in the countryside of poor countries produce virtually no waste at all. They mainly eat the food they grow - they don't buy packaged food. Any leftovers are used to fertilize their next year's crop. People who live in the cities of these countries, however, now have similar throw-away habits to the industrialised world and create huge rubbish dumps. Some poor city dwellers make a living scavenging through these dumps for things to sell.

Our planet is being littered with more and more waste. Wherever people go, they leave litter behind them. Just think - a drink can thrown thoughtlessly out of a car or on to the ground may still be there in 500 years from now if no-one else comes to pick it up. All the waste people create has to go somewhere. Usually it is either burned or buried. Many countries are now running out of places where they can safely bury their rubbish and scientists are worried about the effects of the dangerous chemicals, which are released when waste is burned. Some cities now load their waste aboard ships and send it to other countries or dump it at sea.

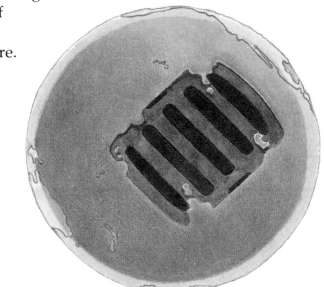

The Earth has become our dustbin.

The rivers and oceans have become our drain.

Most of us don't think about where our waste goes - as long as it goes. It's like brushing dust under the carpet.

To solve the rubbish crisis, we all need to recycle our waste whenever possible. Glass bottles, metal cans and newspapers can all be sent back to factories and turned into new bottles, cans and paper. This means that less waste is produced and we save raw materials.

Almost everything can be recycled - paper, metal, cardboard, glass, cans, old clothes, leftover food. If it can't be recycled, ask yourself if you really need it.

RUINING THE RAINFOREST

Until less than 100 years ago, most of the places that straddle the equator, such as Brazil, central Africa and the East Indies, were covered with vast, wet, steamy forests, known as rainforests. These are nature's greatest triumph. They only cover 6 per cent of the land, but they are home to more than half of all the types of plants and animals on Earth, perhaps as many as 15 million species. Millions of people live there as well. Most of the inhabitants still live very simply, hunting animals such as wild pigs and cutting small clearings to plant crops. But their land is being taken over by outsiders who are clearing the land permanently for crops, timber companies who are cutting down and selling the hardwood trees and cattle ranchers. The destruction of the rainforests could be a disaster both for nature and for the people who live in the forests.

Indicates the regions of tropical rainforests.

Trees are like giant sponges soaking up vast amounts of rainwater. Some water evaporates in the hot sun. The rest passes through the trees to the forest soil.

Plant roots keep moisture in the soil and hold the soil particles in place.

A rainforest is a giant water and weather machine. It needs a lot of rain to grow, but it also creates rain by continually recycling water. Water is stored in the soil, in the trees and even in the air.

When rain falls on the trees most of it lands on leaves, not the ground.

The heat of the Sun makes the raindrops evaporate into the air.

The raindrops are blown many miles, then form new clouds that rain again on the forest.

20

The rainforest is a complex balance of plants and animals. Each one has its part to play in the balance of nature.

It is rather like a stack of tins in a supermarket. The trees and animals which the inhabitants use are like the tins at the top If they are removed, they do not harm the rest.

The main forest is like the tins at the bottom. If they are removed, the whole stack tumbles down. If the forest is cut down, the people, plants and animals in it are destroyed.

If the trees are removed, the rain falls on to the ground and runs into rivers and the sea. It often washes away the forest soils that were held in place by the tree roots. If there are fewer trees to recycle the water, there will be less rain, and the soil will become drier.

Rainforests play an important role in rainfall, not just over the rainforests but over the entire planet. Scientists fear that if we chop down much more of the very large rainforests in Brazil and central Africa, the climate may change all over the world.

Every second, of every minute, of every hour, of every day, an area of rainforest the size of a soccer pitch is destroyed. Every day, one species of animal, insect or plant disappears forever.

Cutting down the trees is like pulling a giant plug in the rain-making cycle. Without trees to store the water, it is lost.

We have found many plants in the rainforests useful as foods or medicines. There may be thousands more waiting to be discovered, but because the rainforests are being destroyed at such a fast rate, we may never find them.

21

THE GREENHOUSE EFFECT

The destruction of the rainforests is changing the balance of gases in the atmosphere. Trees absorb carbon dioxide as they grow. But when they are burned or rot after being cut down, they release carbon dioxide. If carbon dioxide is released faster than it can be absorbed, there will be more carbon dioxide in the air. This will trap more heat from the Sun and add to Earth's natural greenhouse effect.

Burning fossil fuels - oil, coal and gas - also releases carbon dioxide into the atmosphere. These fuels are the remains of ancient forests that grew tens of millions of years ago.

Every tree, every tonne of coal or oil, contains within it trapped carbon. When burned, the carbon is released into the atmosphere as carbon dioxide - just as a balloon releases gas when popped.

About 200 years ago, the first factories were built. At about the same time, the world's population began to increase quickly. To feed, clothe and keep these extra people warm, and to power the factories, forests have been cut down and ever more fossil fuels burned. In those 200 years, the amount of carbon dioxide in the atmosphere has increased by a third.

Earth is in flames. Every year, farmers set the rainforests on fire to clear land to farm. And in industrialised countries, power stations and cars release even more carbon dioxide.

Special sorts of bacteria produce methane. They are found in marshes and bogs, in paddy fields, in waste tips and in the guts of cattle and sheep. Natural gas also contains methane.

Humans have also increased the amount of other 'greenhouse gases' in the atmosphere. One of these is methane. This gas is produced by bugs that live in waste dumps, in wet places such as waterlogged rice fields and in the guts of cattle and sheep. These animals release methane when they fart or belch. As the world grows more rice, raises more cattle, and creates more rubbish dumps, the amount of methane in the air increases. It has doubled in the past 200 years.

CFCs are used either in the making of these things, or to help them work.

Man-made chemicals called chlorofluorocarbons, or CFCs for short, are a third source of greenhouse gases. They have been used in refrigerators, air conditioners, foam plastics and, until recently, in most aerosol spray cans.

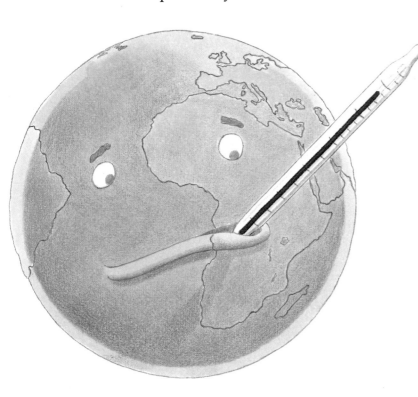

Like a human on a hot summer's day, Earth is over-heating.

As these greenhouse gases build up in the atmosphere, they trap more heat. The result is that the world is likely to become hotter. Scientists call this global warming. It may already be under way. The 1980s were the warmest decade on record around the world. If greenhouse gases are added to the atmosphere at the present ever-rising rate, the global temperature could rise by 4°C by the year 2030.

A WARMER WORLD

You may think that a temperature rise of 4°C worldwide would be nothing much to worry about. However, a drop of 4°C would be enough to take us back to an Ice Age. A rise of 4°C would make the Earth warmer than it has been for the last 100,000 years and would upset the world's climate. Climatologists (people who study the weather) have gathered enough information about changing rainfall and temperatures from around the world to agree the world will get warmer, but they cannot be sure how this will affect each particular part of the planet. In fact, they think that the weather will become more unpredictable.

Global warming is like wrapping an extra blanket around Earth.

In the 1980s, there was all sorts of extreme weather - heatwaves, droughts, floods, tornadoes, hurricanes and typhoons - which some scientists have taken as a sign of global warming. Small changes in the average temperature or rainfall will make extreme events like these more frequent. This could be very damaging. If, for example, an area has a drought for several years running, crops will fail and there will be famine. This is already happening in parts of Africa.

Global warming will be most noticeable in the polar regions. Icecaps will start to melt.

As icecaps melt, sea levels will rise. Places which are close to sea level, such as the Nile and Yangtze deltas, Bangladesh and Florida, will be underwater.

Scientists predict that the warming will not be spread evenly. The tropics will become only a little warmer, but the North and South Poles may become up to 8°C hotter. Any change in the way heat is spread around the world will upset where rain falls and how winds blow.

In a warmer world, more water will evaporate from the oceans, creating more rain and storms near coasts. But further inland, moisture evaporating from soils during hot summers will dry out fields and may cause crops to fail. Two of the major cereal-growing areas, the mid-West of America and the Ukraine in the Soviet Union, are far inland and so are vulnerable. However, warmer weather may help farming in places now too cold to grow good crops, such as Siberia and northern Canada.

Places where much of the world's food is grown could become barren deserts if rains fail and soils dry out.

The oceans will absorb some of the extra heat from the air. But, since water expands as it warms, the sea level will rise. Icecaps and glaciers will melt, adding to the water in the oceans and making sea levels rise further. A rise of 1 metre in the next century would flood coastlines and low-lying land, where millions of people live. Salty water will make the surrounding land unsuitable for growing crops. Many of the world's great cities which are built by the sea, such as New York, London, Shanghai and Sydney, could be flooded.

Spreading deserts and rising tides could leave millions of people hungry and homeless, especially in poor countries. Where will these environmental refugees go?

If the Antarctic icecaps totally melted, the sea level would rise as much as 60 metres. But this would take many hundreds of years.

TROUBLE IN THE AIR

The atmosphere is not only becoming warmer, it is also becoming dirtier. Car fumes are mainly to blame, but so are power stations and factories. The fossil fuels they burn give off dangerous gases, which can cause diseases. The pollution is often worse in summer, when sunlight changes the gases into thin hazy clouds, called smog.

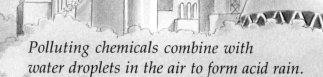

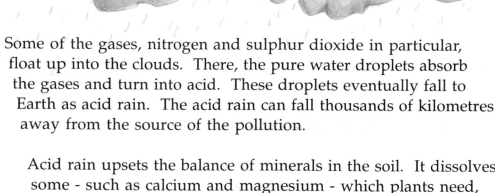

Polluting chemicals combine with water droplets in the air to form acid rain.

Some of the gases, nitrogen and sulphur dioxide in particular, float up into the clouds. There, the pure water droplets absorb the gases and turn into acid. These droplets eventually fall to Earth as acid rain. The acid rain can fall thousands of kilometres away from the source of the pollution.

Acid rain upsets the balance of minerals in the soil. It dissolves some - such as calcium and magnesium - which plants need, but releases other harmful ones, such as aluminium. Trees are badly affected by acid rain. The needles develop yellow spots and drop off; their branches grow thin; the roots are damaged and eventually the trees die.

Both acid rain and aluminium may wash into rivers and lakes, killing some of the water creatures. Some lakes are so acidic that very little lives in them at all.

Millions of conifers in Europe and North America have died as a result of acid rain.

Many countries now produce much less air pollution than they used to. Cleaner power stations are making rain less acid, and new cars with 'catalytic converters' fitted on their exhaust pipes, will also help.

Snails and crayfish are the first to die as water becomes more acidic, followed by salmon and trout. Only eels can live in very acidic water.

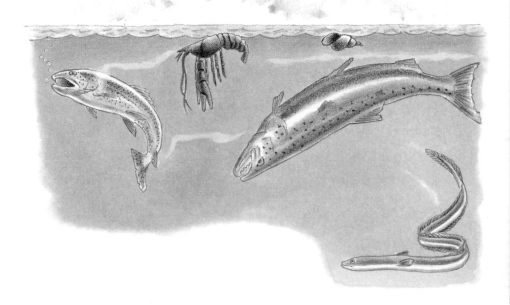

Acid rain is as acidic as lemon juice, and eats away at stone and metal. Millions of pounds are spent each year on repairing damage to ornate cathedral stonework.

Air pollution is also damaging the ozone layer, which shields us from harmful ultraviolet radiation from the Sun. The damage is caused mainly by CFCs.

CFCs were thought to be very safe chemicals because they do not normally burn, decompose or change in any way. Unfortunately, they *are* broken down by ultraviolet light. Sooner or later, the CFCs drift up through the atmosphere until they reach the ozone layer where the ultraviolet radiation is stronger. The radiation breaks up CFCs and chlorine is released. The chlorine reacts with the ozone and destroys it.

In the spring of 1984, scientists discovered a huge hole in the ozone layer over the frozen continent of Antarctica. In 1989, scientists also found a hole over the North Pole. The ozone layer is growing thinner in other places as well.

The hole in the ozone layer is like a crack in Earth's sunglasses, letting through harmful ultraviolet radiation.

The algae which live in the sea are sensitive to ultraviolet radiation and could be killed if the ozone layer thins too much. This would be disastrous for other sea creatures which eat algae. The entire food chain would be disrupted.

Now that people realize the damage done by CFCs, some countries have banned their use and asked factories to stop producing them. Most aerosol spray cans no longer contain CFCs, and scientists are looking for ways to replace them in other products.

TIME FOR ACTION

Can you now see how all the pieces fit together? Earth is like a jigsaw. The land, sea, air and living things are all connected. By poisoning the water, destroying soils, killing off animals and plants, burning forests and polluting the air, it is as if we are throwing away some of the jigsaw pieces. That affects every part of the planet.

But we need not despair. If we imagine the entire history of Earth so far lasting a single day, then human-like creatures have been around for less than a minute, and Homo sapiens for less than a second. Looked at that way, we are just another nuisance for a planet that has survived all sorts of disasters.

Nature will survive. Even in the most polluted cities or rivers, some things can still live. What we have to worry about is whether we are making Earth unfit for *us* to live on. Will the greenhouse effect turn our planet into an unbearable hot desert? Are we destroying the species of plants and animals that could feed and cure us in the future? Can we save the ozone layer which protects us?

Humans may be the most destructive species on the planet, but we do have one great advantage over other creatures. We can become aware of what we are doing to our environment and can work out ways to save it. Many countries are already cleaning up their rivers and stopping the pollution that causes acid rain. The world's governments joined together to act quickly once there was scientific proof that pollution was creating a hole in the ozone layer. There are plans for international action to halt the destruction of the rainforests and to find ways to slow down the greenhouse effect.

But we can't just leave things to governments. We must all help. You may think that your individual action can't possibly make a difference to the crisis facing Earth. But it *can*. Remember, many of the problems we face now were caused by the individual actions of millions of people all over the Earth. So each of our actions helps improve the environment. If each of us does what he or she can, Earth will be safe for you and future generations to enjoy. It's up to us.

The first step is to get more information on the issues which concern you the most. Below is a list of some organisations you might want to contact or join. Read other books on environmental issues; try your local library or bookshop.

Friends of the Earth
26 Underwood Street
London
N1 7JQ
Can supply information on environmental issues of all kinds. Their junior branch is Earth Action - for 14-25 year olds. Has local branches.

Waste Watch
26 Bedford Square
London
WC1 3HU
Can provide information on recycling. A 'Dustbin Pack' is available for primary teachers.

Steel Can Recycling Information Bureau
Kingsgate House
536 Kings Road
London
SW10 0TE
Can supply information on how metal is recycled.

Greenpeace
Greenpeace House
Canonbury Villas
London
N1 2PN
Campaigns on environmental issues worldwide.

RSPB
The Lodge
Sandy
Beds
SG19 2DL
Campaigns for birds and other wildlife worldwide. Its junior branch is The Young Ornithologists Club.

Woodland Trust
Autumn Park
Dysart Road
Grantham
Lincs
NG31 6LL
Campaigns to save English woodlands. Can supply information on this.

Watch Trust for Environmental Education
22 The Green
Nettleham
Lincoln
LN2 2NR
A wildlife and environment club for children and their families. Organises activities for children at a local level.

World Wide Fund for Nature
Panda House
Weyside Park
Catteshall Lane
Godalming
Surrey
GU7 1XR
Campaigns for nature worldwide. Can provide information about this. Has a junior branch.

The Soil Association
86 Colston Street
Bristol
BS1 5BB
Can supply information on organic food and farming.
[Please send a large SAE.]

National Centre for Alternative Technology
Llwyngwern Quarry
Machynlleth
Powys
SY20 9AZ
Can provide information on environment-friendly technology.
[Please enclose an A4 SAE.]

The second step is to do what you can. Look in your Yellow Pages for details of people who can recycle paper, metal or glass, for instance. Why not set up a recycling scheme at school? Save energy at home by turning off lights you don't need, or walking or cycling instead of relying on a car. Look out for local environmental events in the library or local paper.

Remember, the more you do to help Earth, the greener and safer it will become for everyone!

A David Bennett Book

For Harriet, Joseph and Eleanor
F.P.
For Jane
I.W.

First published in 1991 by
Kingfisher Books,
Grisewood & Dempsey Ltd,
Elsley House, 24-30 Great Titchfield Street,
London, W1P 7AD

Text copyright © 1991 Fred Pearce
Illustrations copyright © 1991 Ian Winton

Editor: Ruth Thomson
Assistant Editor: Karen Filsell
Art Director: Steve Avery
Designer: Roger Hands

BRITISH LIBRARY CATALOGUING IN PUBLICATION DATA
Pearce, Fred
Ian and Fred's big green book.
1. Environment
I. Title II. Winton, Ian
333.7
ISBN 0 86272 661 1

Created and produced by
David Bennett Books Ltd,
94 Victoria Street, St Albans,
Herts, AL1 3TG

Typesetting by Type City
Production by Imago
Printed in Hong Kong